Finding Style

How to Use Today's Versatile Jewelry-Making Components

FindingStyle

How to Use Today's Versatile Jewelry-Making Components

Irina Miech

KALMBACH BOOKS

Kalmbach Books
21027 Crossroads Circle
Waukesha, Wisconsin 53186
www.Kalmbach.com/Books

Published in 2014
18 17 16 15 14   1 2 3 4 5

Manufactured in the United States of America

ISBN: 978-1-62700-058-1
EISBN: 978-1-62700-059-8

Editor: Karin Van Voorhees
Art Director: Lisa Bergman
Photographers: William Zuback and James Forbes

Publisher's Cataloging-In-Publication Data

Miech, Irina.
    Finding style : how to use today's versatile jewelry-making components / Irina Miech.
      pages : color illustrations ; cm
    Issued also as an ebook.
    ISBN: 978-1-62700-058-1
    1. Jewelry making—Handbooks, manuals, etc. 2. Metal-work—Handbooks, manuals, etc. 3. Leather-work—Handbooks, manuals, etc. I. Title.
TT212 .M54344 2014
745.594/2

Contents

16 Bezels and Settings Collection

Featuring Swarovski rivolis and filigree bezel settings

28 Gear Collection

Featuring gear components, crystals, and jump rings

Your Style is Your Story

Today, jewelry makers can choose from a vast array of components, findings, and techniques. Beading is no longer limited to just beads—it has evolved tremendously in the last decade. It is easier than ever to finish projects professionally and elegantly. We have new techniques that broaden design options, and there are many creative interpretations of traditional methods and materials.

I wrote this book to introduce these new specialized findings, components, and techniques, as well as creatively broaden the way they are used. Some familiar basics are included, but these concepts are expanded. You'll learn how to make your own clasps and earring wires, and how to use manufactured components in unexpected ways to elevate your designs.

Artists evolve through exploring a series of related designs, which allows both artistic vision and technical skills to grow. I've presented these projects in collections for this reason. You'll find different ways of working with similar materials in each one, and build your skills and your imagination as you go.

Jewelry makers tell a story through the work they create; making these projects will help you explore your own voice. For example, by using certain textures, hammering, including words, and shaping metal, you can create a unique and personal expression. Using the right components, such as a handmade clasp or bail, helps you create a complementary flow to a design and make it your own.

This book has something for everyone, from the beginner hoping to learn the basics of beading to the more experienced designer interested in learning to think as a three-dimensional artist and to innovate both with purchased findings as well as with those of her own creation. Finding your own style is the key to being a successful jewelry designer and this book is meant to help inspire you to do just that.

I hope that after exploring the different projects and the way that I have used findings, beads, and various metal components, you—the designer—will be encouraged to explore the many possibilities and see how findings and design methods are open to innovation and interpretation. Your style is your story. Enjoy the journey and bring your unique artistic voice into the tale you tell with your jewelry designs.

Irina Miech

HOW TO USE THIS BOOK ▼

Use the visual tool and findings guide to see an overview of the most common supplies used in this book. Each chapter begins with a specialized overview of all the materials you'll use for that jewelry collection and a custom Basics tutorial that teaches new or unique techniques used in those projects. Materials, tools, and supplies lists for each collection are grouped at the end of the chapter for easy reference.

New Tools and Findings

Featuring pliers, cutters, hole punches, and more

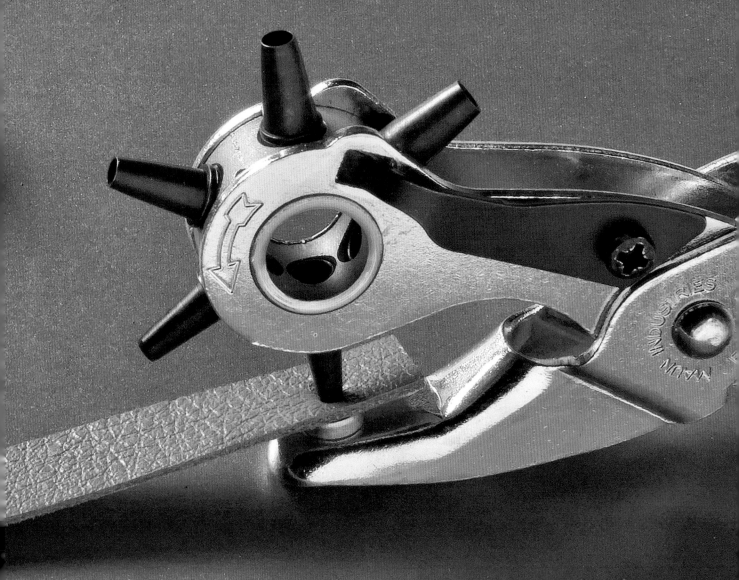

TOOLS

Chainnose pliers bend and manipulate wire in small spaces.

Roundnose pliers make loops, rounded curves, and start spirals.

Flatnose pliers bend and hold wire.

Nylon-jaw pliers straighten kinks out of wire.

Flexible beading wire cutters cut flexible beading wire. Some side cutters can cut flexible beading wire as well.

Side cutters are used to cut wire.

Metal shears cut sheet metal.

Tool Magic coats the jaws of pliers with a rubbery substance to help prevent damage to wire, and is helpful for beginners.

A **metal ring mandrel** is for ring shaping and sizing.

Choose **files** based on the end result required. A flat file is for filing edges of metal components.

A **needle stylus** marks flat leather for hole placement.

A **chasing hammer** has two sides: one is almost flat but slightly rounded, and the other has a ball and is used for texturing.

Use a **brass hammer** or a deadblow hammer to strike steel punches such as those for dapping, texture, or letters.

Use a **riveting hammer** to strike the top of a rivet when setting.

Texturing hammers add texture or create patterns on metal.

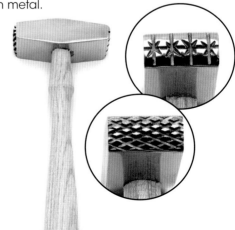

Ergonomically designed tools have comfortable grips that reduce hand stress. Because I work with tools on a daily basis, I make it a point to use ergonomically designed tools as much as possible.

Crimping pliers are used with flexible beading wire and crimp tubes to attach clasps or other findings.

Bail-making pliers create equally sized loops or curves in metal.

A **EuroPower hole punch** punches holes of multiple diameters in metal and leather.

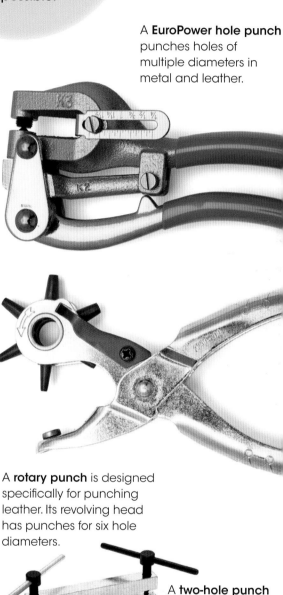

A **rotary punch** is designed specifically for punching leather. Its revolving head has punches for six hole diameters.

A **two-hole punch** has two different diameters and is for punching metal and leather.

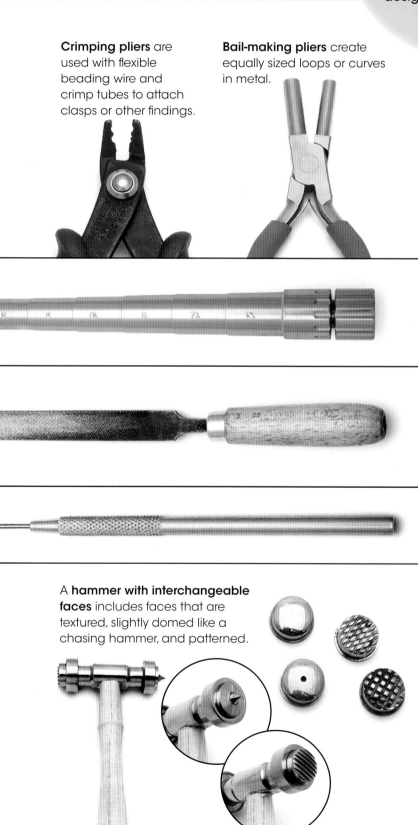

A **hammer with interchangeable faces** includes faces that are textured, slightly domed like a chasing hammer, and patterned.

Hole-punch pliers punch small holes in metal and leather.

13

Use a **wooden dapping block** with a chasing hammer, metal punches, or wooden punches, and make domed metal disks or components.

Punches pair with a dapping block to dome metal.

Use a **dapping block** with dapping punches and a deadblow hammer to dome metal disks or components (sometimes it is flat on the other side and can be used as a bench block).

Use an **agate burnisher** for the final step in setting a stone or a rivoli in a bezel setting.

A **bench block** is a smooth metal surface to hammer against.

An **anvil** is for hammering or riveting metal. To hammer an unconventional shape, or for a smaller working area, use a horn.

A **cup bur** is an inverted diamond file used to round wire ends.

SUPPLIES

Adhesive secures thread when knotted and also secures pinch ends, end caps, and clasps.

Liver of sulfur is a chemical that adds patina to silver and copper. Use polishing pads to remove some of the finish to enhance contrast and bring out detail.

FINDINGS

Headpins and **ball headpins** are lengths of wire with a head or a ball at one end, which acts as a stopper to hold beads in place. Some headpins have decorative ends containing a crystal, a gemstone, or silver granulation. The most common headpin gauges are 22 and 24. I use 24 gauge or smaller for making wrapped loops, and 22 gauge or larger for plain loops.

Earring wires can vary in design, both aesthetically and in function. The most common are French hooks, but there are many other styles available.

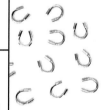

Jump rings are available in many different sizes, both soldered and unsoldered, or open. They are essential for many jewelry designs. Some sources measure jump rings by the outside diameter, others by the inside diameter. In this book I have referred to the outside diameter in all material lists.

Chain is a wonderful element for any jewelry designer, from the tiniest link to the largest. It adds movement to designs and can also form an adjustable clasp when paired with a hook (called an extender chain).

Crimp locks are a great new alternative to traditional crimp tubes and can be used with flexible beading wire.

Clasps are essential, but should also be considered a design element—select one that enhances or complements the piece. A variety of clasps are available, such as toggles, hooks, lobster claws, and many others. In addition, you can make your own clasp out of wire.

Wire guards (also called cable thimbles) have a rigid, pre-curved horseshoe shape to cradle and protect the flexible beading wire that is attached to a metal component such as a clasp. Wire guards also give a piece a more polished, professional finish.

Crimp tubes and beads connect clasps and other findings to flexible beading wire. Some crimps are used with crimping pliers.

Pinch ends are used when finishing leather, SilverSilk chain, or multiple strand necklaces and bracelets.

Two-part rivets are used to layer metal components or connect them to flat leather.

Flexible beading wire is comprised of several strands of stainless steel wire encased in a nylon coating. There are different sizes available. It's used with crimp beads or crimp locks and does not knot well.

Wire is an essential component for many jewelry designs. It is available in multiple gauges and metal finishes.

Bezels and Settings Collection

BASICS

FINDINGS YOU'LL USE ▼

1 crystal rivoli
2 crystal ring
3 flat-backed crystal
4 cabochon or flat gemstone
5 two-part rivets
6 flat filigree
7 round silver-filled wire
8 jump rings
9 bezel setting with one
  or four loops
10 freeform glass pendant
11 buttons with shanks
12 flat leather
13 hinged bail
14 toggle clasp
15 leaf-shaped charm
16 flat leather end
17 flat spacers
18 metal blanks

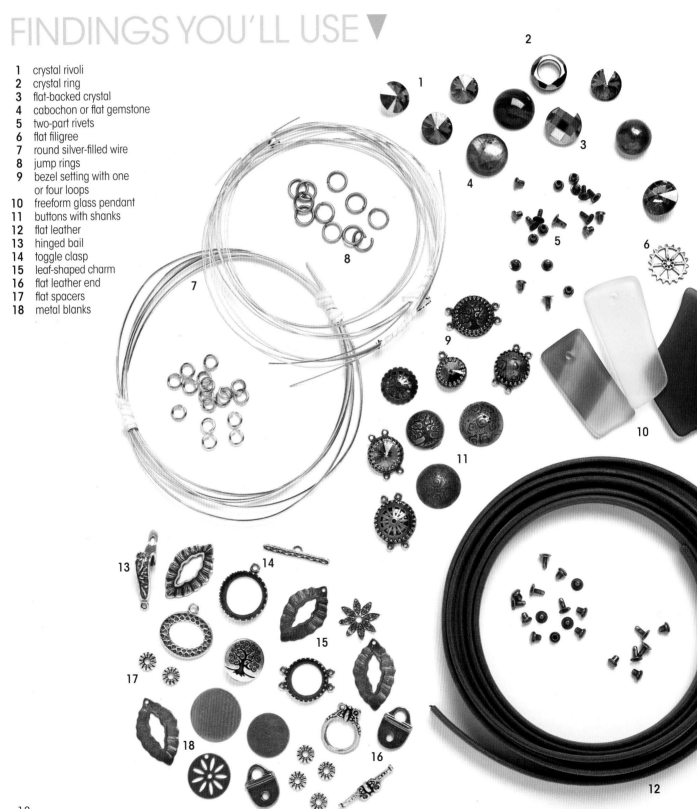

set a rivoli in a bezel

Place a rivoli in a bezel setting. Use the tips of flatnose pliers to fold down the bezel prongs (start by bending opposite sides, such as 12 o'clock/6 o'clock, and then 3 o'clock/9 o'clock).

open and close loops or jump rings

Hold the loop or jump ring with two pairs of chainnose pliers or chainnose and roundnose pliers, as shown.

To open the loop or jump ring, bring one pair of pliers toward you and push the other pair away. String materials on the open loop or jump ring. Reverse the steps to close the open loop or jump ring.

make a domed cap

Place a gear, filigree component, or metal blank in the largest concavity of a dapping block. Place the largest dapping punch on the component and strike with a deadblow hammer. (It's best to lightly dap the component multiple times, adjusting the punch to round out the shape evenly.)

If you're looking for a deeper curve, move the component to the next concavity and use the corresponding dapping punch. Continue this process until you're satisfied with the depth of the curve in your piece.

make a domed base from a button

Cut the shank from the back of a button.

Carefully dome the component using a dapping block and punch, as in "make a domed cap."

add patina with liver of sulfur

Dilute a few drops of gel or a pea-sized chunk of liver of sulfur in a small bowl of warm water. Immerse the metal component until it reaches the desired color. Rinse in cold water and dry. Use an abrasive pad to polish the component, leaving color in the textured areas.

Crystal Botanica Earrings

These wonderfully simple bezel components make it easy to set a variety of stones and cabochons, including Swarovski rivolis. Note the contrasts in this design: The organic leaf stampings with their antiqued brass color become a dark backdrop, which pairs beautifully with the brighter silver of the bezel. The sparkling rivoli jewel floats in the center like a dewdrop.

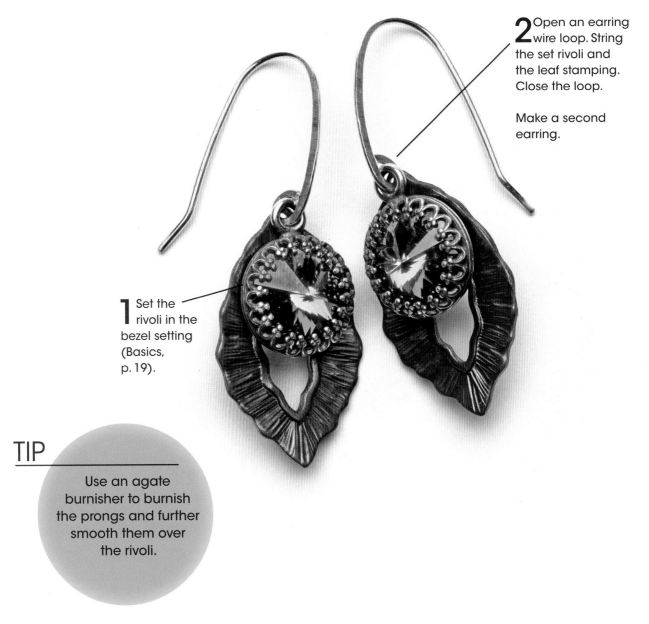

2 Open an earring wire loop. String the set rivoli and the leaf stamping. Close the loop.

Make a second earring.

1 Set the rivoli in the bezel setting (Basics, p. 19).

TIP

Use an agate burnisher to burnish the prongs and further smooth them over the rivoli.

Layered
Filigree Ring

Designing on a small scale is always a fun challenge. When you only have a limited space to work with, such as a single bezel on a ring, it really helps to narrow your focus. To personalize this ring setting, I added dimension by combining two layered elements. I attached jump rings on the sides of the shank to give the ring more visual texture.

Use a dapping block to create a curve in a gear component so it fits in the bezel opening on the ring (Basics, p. 19). Place the flatback crystal in the bezel setting, and layer the gear component over it. Secure the setting (Basics, p. 19). Attach a brass-colored textured jump ring for an interesting detail (Close-up).

CLOSE-UP ▼

Connect a textured jump ring to the ring shank with two pairs of jump rings, then repeat on the other side.

Eclectic Treasure Bracelet

Because this design started with several uniform settings, I felt that the way to make it interesting was to vary the color and texture of each bezeled component. Beyond stones and rivolis, what else I could capture? Each new material was a bit of a puzzle to solve: For example, how could a blank or a button fit?

1 Set a cosmic ring, a mabé pearl, and a stone cabochon in a bezel (Basics, p. 19).

4 Make a textured blank component (Close-up). Place in a bezel and set the bezel (Basics, p. 19).

5 Use jump rings to connect the components and attach a toggle clasp.

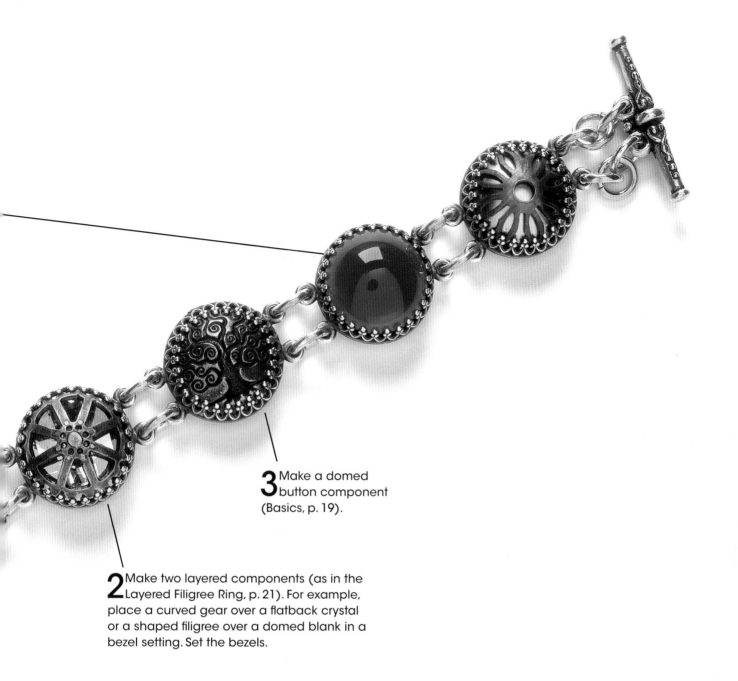

3 Make a domed button component (Basics, p. 19).

2 Make two layered components (as in the Layered Filigree Ring, p. 21). For example, place a curved gear over a flatback crystal or a shaped filigree over a domed blank in a bezel setting. Set the bezels.

CLOSE-UP ▼

textured blank component
Use metal punches and texture hammers to texture one side of a blank. Gain control by striking the texture hammer with a deadblow hammer.

Dome the blank in a dapping block, textured side down.

Use liver of sulfur to add patina (Basics, p. 19).

Chic Bezeled Jewel Bracelet

This bracelet has an elegant, clean style that really

appeals to me. I love the look of the bezeled rivoli

against the matte texture of the leather.

The clasp

complements

the bezel

component and

echos the filigree style. When you are

designing a piece with very few elements,

each element must create visual harmony.

STEP BY STEP

1 Set the rivoli in the bezel setting (Basics, p. 19). Use jump rings to attach each of the loops on the bezeled rivoli component to one of the holes in each of the two-strand spacers.

TIP

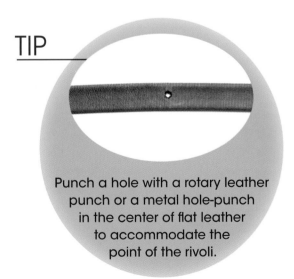

Punch a hole with a rotary leather punch or a metal hole-punch in the center of flat leather to accommodate the point of the rivoli.

TIP

For more instruction on setting two-part rivets, see the Close-up on p. 51.

2 Punch a hole in the center of the flat leather to accommodate the rivoli point (Tip, p. 24).

3 Center the assembly on the flat leather so that the rivoli point rests in the hole. Use a needle stylus or a marker to mark the placement of the open loops on the two-strand spacers.

Use the large end of the two-hole punch to punch the first set of holes.

4 Stack the bottom of a two-part rivet, the leather, an open two-strand spacer loop, and the top of the rivet, then carefully hammer until the rivet holds firmly. Repeat for the adjacent two-strand spacer.

Attach the other end of the assembly in the same way.

5 Use a two-hole punch to punch a hole approximately 5mm from each end of the bracelet.

6 Stack the bottom of a two-part rivet, a strap end, and the top of the rivet so that the edge of the strap end is lined up with the end of the leather. Place on the bench block so that the protruding edge hangs over the edge of the bench block and hammer until the rivet holds firmly. Repeat on the other end.

7 Use double jump rings to attach the toggle ring to one end and three sets of double jump rings to attach the toggle bar to the other end.

Moods of the Ocean Pendant

I love contrast between texture and color—here, the dark background of organic velvety matte glass lets the chatoyant beauty of the cabochon shine. The silver spiral adds movement and visual interest, and draws the eye down the expanse of glass. Just for fun, I riveted a spacer to the spiral.

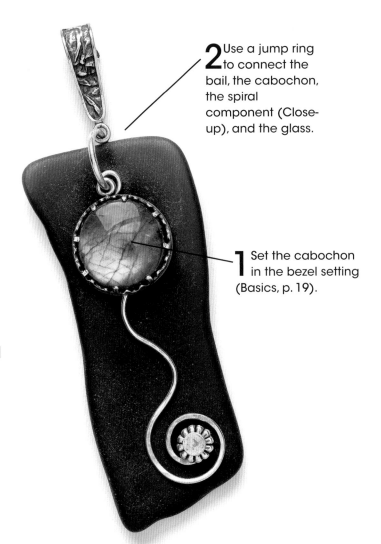

2 Use a jump ring to connect the bail, the cabochon, the spiral component (Close-up), and the glass.

1 Set the cabochon in the bezel setting (Basics, p. 19).

CLOSE-UP ▼

spiral component
Use roundnose pliers to make an approximately 3mm round loop at the end of a wire.

Use chainnose pliers to grasp the loop. Create a loose spiral by spiraling the wire by hand.

Use large bail-making pliers to create a soft zigzag not quite the length of the glass component.

Use roundnose pliers to make a loop at the end of the wire.

Hammer the spiral component with a chasing hammer.

Stack the bottom of a two-part rivet, the open loop in the center of the spiral, the flat spacer, and the top of the rivet. Carefully hammer with a riveting hammer until the rivet holds firmly.

MATERIALS

Crystal Botanica Earrings
page 20

2 10mm rivolis

2 10mm one-loop bezel settings

2 15x26mm leaf stampings

Pair of earring wires

Tools & Supplies

Chainnose pliers

Flatnose pliers

Optional: agate burnisher

Chic Bezeled Jewel Bracelet
page 24

14mm rivoli

14mm four-loop bezel setting

4 2-strand findings with large holes

6 two-part rivets

10–12 5mm jump rings

2 strap ends

Toggle clasp

6-in. 10mm-wide flat leather

Tools & Supplies

Chainnose pliers

Flatnose pliers

Riveting hammer

Bench block

Two-hole punch or EuroPower hole punch

Needle stylus or fine-tip marker

Optional: agate burnisher

Layered Filigree Ring
page 21

14mm flatback chessboard circle crystal

16mm gear component

14mm filigree bezel ring

8 4mm jump rings

2 6mm textured rings

Tools & Supplies

Chainnose pliers

Flatnose pliers

Dapping block and dapping punches

Deadblow hammer

Optional: agate burnisher

Moods of the Ocean Pendant
page 26

16mm round labradorite cabochon

2¾x1¼ in. flat matte freeform glass pendant

16mm filigree setting

12mm jump ring

Two-part rivet

7mm flat spacer bead

6x22mm bail

6-in. 18-gauge round sterling wire

Tools & Supplies

Chainnose pliers

Roundnose pliers

Flatnose pliers

Large bail-making pliers

Side cutters

Riveting hammer

Chasing hammer

Bench block

Optional: agate burnisher

Eclectic Treasure Bracelet
page 22

16mm gear component

16mm filigree flower component

16mm copper blank

16mm silvertone blank

15mm button

14mm Swarovski cosmic ring

14mm mabé pearl

14mm flatback component

14mm round stone cabochon

7 four-loop bezel components

20 6mm jump rings

Two-strand toggle clasp

Tools & Supplies

2 pairs of chainnose pliers or flatnose and chainnose pliers

Side cutters

Dapping block and dapping punches

Bench block

Deadblow hammer

Texturing hammers

Decorative metal punches

Liver of sulfur

Abrasive pad

Optional: agate burnisher

Gear
Collection

Featuring gear components, crystals, and jump rings

BASICS

FINDINGS YOU'LL USE ▼

1   braided leather cord
2   crystals—bicone
3   gears
4   bail
5   cord ends—SilverSilk
6   cord ends—leather
7   SilverSilk
8   toggle clasp
9   crystals—round, rivoli, 9x6mm
10 round leather cord
11 28-gauge craft wire

wrapped loop dangle

1 Make sure you have at least 1¼ in. (3.2cm) of wire above the bead. With the tip of chainnose pliers, grasp the wire directly above the bead. Bend the wire (above the pliers) into a right angle.

2 Using roundnose pliers, position the jaws in the bend.

3 Bring the wire over the top jaw of the roundnose pliers.

4 Reposition the pliers' lower jaw snugly into the loop. Curve the wire downward around the bottom of the roundnose pliers. This is the first half of a wrapped loop.

5 Position the chainnose pliers' jaws across the loop.

6 Wrap the wire around the wire stem, covering the stem between the loop and the top bead. Trim the excess wire and press the cut end close to the wraps with chainnose pliers.

lark's head knot

Fold a cord in half and lay it over a ring, loop, etc. Bring the ends through the ring from back to front, then through the fold and tighten.

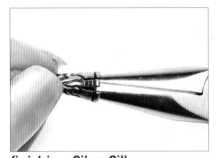  

finishing SilverSilk

Open a pinch end with chainnose pliers.

Insert an end of SilverSilk chain into the pinch end as far as it will go.

Use chainnose pliers to firmly close the pinch end, making certain to push in the prong sides.

finishing leather cord

Insert leather ends into the pinch ends and squeeze the petals of the pinch ends tightly with nylon-jaw pliers (you may need to open the pinch ends using chainnose pliers as shown in "finishing SilverSilk").

TIP

Before finishing with end caps, wrap the cut leather ends with wire to prevent fraying.

more about end caps

Use end caps for a professional polish on any cut surface. Dab with glue before inserting into an end cap for added security.

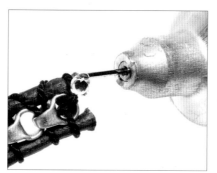

working with wire

Wire comes in many different gauges, or thicknesses. The larger the number, the thinner the wire. In this chapter, you'll use a very thin 28-gauge wire to "sew" components together. When working with thinner wire, you need to be careful to keep it from kinking. Work slowly, work with a shorter piece, and use your non-dominant hand to guide the wire as it comes off the spool or coil.

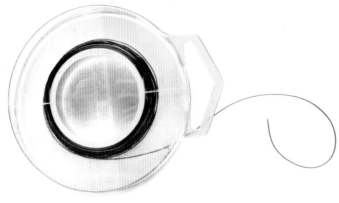

Vintage Gears Necklace

I love blending styles. For this necklace, the antique color of the brass and the balance of the elements results in an Art Deco look, while the gears bring in a touch of Steampunk. The dark jewel tones complement the color of the brass.

7 Use a single 5mm jump ring to connect a hook to one end. Use a single 5mm jump ring to connect an extender chain to the other end. Make a wrapped loop dangle with a 4mm bicone crystal, connecting it to the end of the extender chain before you complete the wraps.

TIP

Find wrapped loop dangle instructions on p. 31.

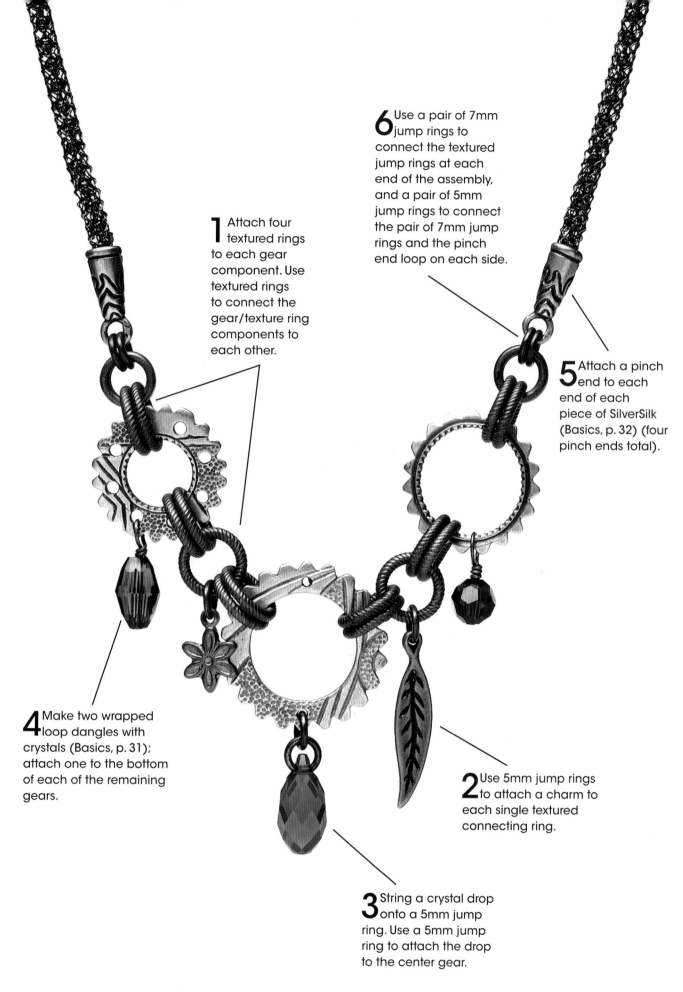

1 Attach four textured rings to each gear component. Use textured rings to connect the gear/texture ring components to each other.

6 Use a pair of 7mm jump rings to connect the textured jump rings at each end of the assembly, and a pair of 5mm jump rings to connect the pair of 7mm jump rings and the pinch end loop on each side.

5 Attach a pinch end to each end of each piece of SilverSilk (Basics, p. 32) (four pinch ends total).

4 Make two wrapped loop dangles with crystals (Basics, p. 31); attach one to the bottom of each of the remaining gears.

2 Use 5mm jump rings to attach a charm to each single textured connecting ring.

3 String a crystal drop onto a 5mm jump ring. Use a 5mm jump ring to attach the drop to the center gear.

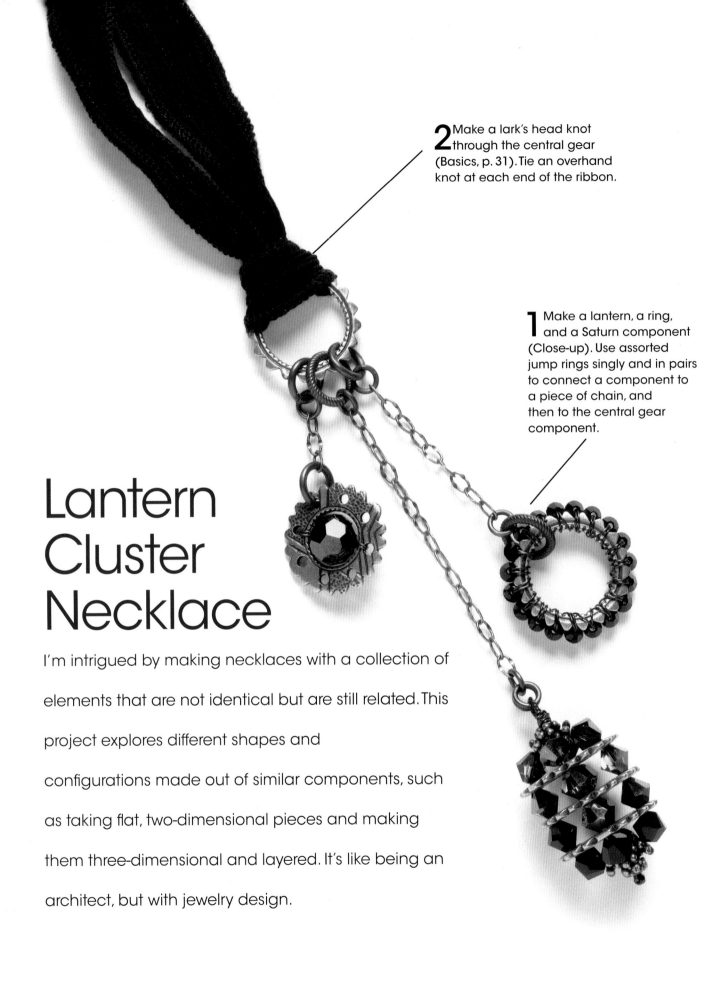

2 Make a lark's head knot through the central gear (Basics, p. 31). Tie an overhand knot at each end of the ribbon.

1 Make a lantern, a ring, and a Saturn component (Close-up). Use assorted jump rings singly and in pairs to connect a component to a piece of chain, and then to the central gear component.

Lantern Cluster Necklace

I'm intrigued by making necklaces with a collection of elements that are not identical but are still related. This project explores different shapes and configurations made out of similar components, such as taking flat, two-dimensional pieces and making them three-dimensional and layered. It's like being an architect, but with jewelry design.

CLOSE-UP ▼

lantern component

String two 8-in. pieces of wire through a 2mm crystal, and then string all four ends through the thick spacer.

Separate the four ends and string a daisy spacer and a 5mm bicone crystal onto each end.

String each wire end through a hole in a gear component, positioning them so they are equidistant from each other (since there are eight holes in each component, you will be stringing through every other hole).

String a single 5mm bicone onto each wire, then string the wire ends through a gear component. Repeat until you have strung through three components and four layers of 5mm crystals.

String a daisy spacer and a 4mm crystal onto each wire.

String all four wires through a daisy spacer.

Twist all four wires together using flatnose and chainnose pliers.

Make a wrapped loop with the twisted wire. Trim and tuck in the ends.

ring component

String a 22-in. piece of wire through a 4mm crystal, leaving an approximately 3-in. tail. Position the crystal at the top and between the two rings (the notches in the two rings should line up).

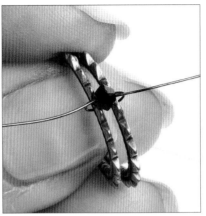

String the long/working end of the wire through the large opening in the rings, and string the wire through the same crystal again.

String the wire through the two rings again, string a crystal, and position the crystal in the next set of notches. Again, string the wire through the ring and back through the crystal just added.

Continue to add crystals, always stringing twice through each crystal.

When you have gone entirely around the ring, and as you are adding your last crystal, string the wire through it and place it in the remaining set of notches. Use the opposite end of the wire (the tail) to string through the same crystal.

Finish by wrapping both ends around an adjacent wire. Trim and tuck them in toward the gear component.

Saturn component

String a 4-in. piece of wire through an 8mm crystal.

String both ends of the wire through opposite holes in the gear.

String between the crystal and the gear and then string back through the same holes in the gear again.

Trim the wire, leaving about 4mm of wire on each side, and use chainnose pliers to tuck the wire ends into the crystal.

Vintage Gears Earrings

These earrings are simple and fun with just a few jump rings and a splash of color. They complement the Vintage Gears Necklace—I isolated a single color from the necklace and carried it to the earrings for an elegant and contemporary coordinating look.

3 Connect a 7mm ring to the remaining pair of textured jump rings and an earring wire. Make a second earring.

1 Attach four textured rings to each gear component.

2 Make a wrapped loop dangle (Basics, p. 31) with a 6mm round crystal and attach it to one pair of textured jump rings.

Chain & Gears Bracelet

I'm always trying to weave different designs and elements together, and this was a fun challenge—to combine the popular look of a wrap bracelet with a bit of Steampunk. Reinterpreting and reinventing both styles and adding one thing to another creates a new look.

1 Attach the leather to the gear component with a lark's head knot (Basics, p. 31). Make the chain and leather strip (Close-up).

3 Assemble the bracelet using two three-jump-ring segments to attach each of the components and each half of the clasp.

CLOSE-UP ▼

chain and leather strip

Slip the end of the silk cord into the lark's head knot in the leather and then tie a knot in the silk cord.

Line up the bicycle chain between the two leather strands. Use the needle attached to the silk cord to go over one of the leather strands, through the vertical link of the chain, around the other leather strand, and back through the same chain link on the opposite side of the bracelet.

Bring the silk cord back over the first leather strand and go through the second vertical link of the chain. Go over the leather strand and back through the link. Continue this pattern until you have gone through all of the vertical chain links on both sides and have gotten to the opposite end of the chain.

Go through the last/horizontally positioned link of the chain several times in a figure 8 pattern.

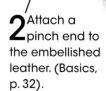

2 Attach a pinch end to the embellished leather. (Basics, p. 32).

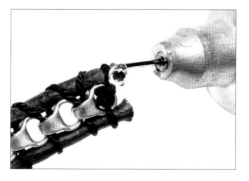

Wrap the silk cord around both ends of the leather and through the last/final chain link, then tie a knot. Use a drop of glue to secure both knots of the silk cord. Let the glue dry.

3 Use jump rings to attach a chain on each end and the clasp to one chain end. String a 6mm bicone onto a headpin and attach it to the other chain end with a wrapped loop.

2 Use 28-gauge wire to tightly wrap each end of the braided leather. Attach a pinch end to each end of the braided leather (Basics, p. 32).

Caged Jewel Necklace

I'm always intrigued by flat components with multiple

holes because they have so many creative possibilities.

Once I began experimenting with these gears,

I discovered they were perfect for layering, and I could

set a rivoli in between them. This caged jewel

makes a simple yet elegant centerpiece

for a braided leather necklace.

1 Make a caged rivoli pendant (Close-up). String the sliding bail onto the braided leather, and use jump rings to attach the pinch bail loop.

CLOSE-UP ▼

caged rivoli

String the wire through a hole in the gear component, a seed bead, and a gear component.

Wrap the wire around the edge of the gear and string it back through all three components. Repeat.

At this point, you should be able to see two passes of wire around the outside edge of the gear.

Bend both ends of the wire toward each other. Trim the wire ends half-way between the gears.

Use chainnose pliers to tuck in the ends.

Skip one hole and then follow the same steps to make a second set of wraps.

Place the rivoli between the two gear components and center it. Make two more sets of wraps, as before.

Use flatnose pliers to squeeze the sides of the pinch bail, pushing the prongs through the corresponding holes on the caged rivoli component.

MATERIALS

Vintage Gears Necklace
page 34

12x6mm top-drilled Swarovski crystal

9x6mm Swarovski crystal

6mm Swarovski round crystal

4mm Swarovski bicone crystal

5x20mm leaf charm

7mm flower charm

22mm textured gear

18mm textured gear

17mm textured gear

14 9mm textured jump rings

4 7mm jump rings

10 5mm jump rings

3 24-gauge headpins

Hook clasp

4 13x4mm pinch ends

2 7-in. pieces of SilverSilk chain

2-in. extender chain

Tools & Supplies

Chainnose pliers

Roundnose pliers

Flatnose pliers

Side cutters

Lantern Cluster Necklace
page 36

8mm Swarovski round crystal

16 5mm Swarovski bicone crystals

19 3mm Swarovski bicone crystals

9 2mm Swarovski round crystals

4mm thick spacer

9 4mm daisy spacers

3 18mm ring gears

4 17mm eight-hole gears

2 9mm textured jump rings

3 7mm jump rings

7 5mm jump rings

Chain cut into a 1¾-, 1-, and ½-in. piece

28-gauge craft wire cut into a 4-, two 8-, and a 22-in. piece

36 in. silk ribbon

Tools & Supplies

Chainnose pliers

Roundnose pliers

Flatnose pliers

Side cutters

Vintage Gears Earrings
page 39

2 6mm Swarovski round crystals

2 18mm textured gears

8 9mm textured jump rings

2 7mm jump rings

2 24-gauge headpins

Pair of earring wires

Tools & Supplies

Chainnose pliers

Flatnose pliers

Roundnose pliers

Side cutters

Chain & Gears Bracelet
page 40

17mm gear
18mm gear
3–3½-in. bicycle chain
8–10-in. leather cord
Silk cord with an attached needle
14x5mm pinch end
18 5mm jump rings
Two-strand toggle clasp

Tools & Supplies
Scissors
Chainnose pliers
Flatnose pliers
G-S Hypo Cement Glue

Caged Jewel Necklace
page 42

10mm rivoli
6mm bicone crystal
4 11º nickel-plated brass seed beads
2 17mm eight-hole gears
2 6mm jump rings
3 5mm jump rings
6 4-in. pieces of 28-gauge wire
Headpin
2 large pinch ends to fit braided leather
Sliding bail
Pinch bail
Hook clasp
12 in. 5mm braided leather
Cable chain cut into a 2- and a 4-in. piece

Tools & Supplies
Chainnose pliers and flatnose pliers or
2 pairs of chainnose pliers
Roundnose pliers
Side cutters
Nylon-jaw pliers

Rivets and Buttons Collection

Featuring metal buttons and two-part rivets

BASICS

FINDINGS YOU'LL USE ▼

1 two-part rivet
2 spacers
3 bead caps and round metal beads
4 strap end
5 pure leaf crystal pendant
6 helix, De-Art, and Ellipse crystal pendants
7 hook clasp
8 bail
9 center-drilled metal flowers
10 metal buttons
11 crystal rings
12 flat leather

securing two-part rivets

1 Place the bottom of the rivet on the bench block.

2 Punch a hole in the item to be riveted, and push the bottom rivet through the hole.

3 Place the top of the rivet onto the bottom rivet and apply a little pressure until it engages.

4 Hold the riveting hammer perpendicular to the piece and use it to hammer the rivet until the rivet holds firmly.

attach a flat leather ending

Punch a hole 5mm from the end of the flat leather. Using the depth of the punch is a good gauge for the placement of the hole.

Push the bottom rivet through the back of the flat leather and place on a bench block.

Place the flat leather ending over the rivet.

Place the top of the rivet over the bottom rivet and place on a bench block. Hammer to complete the connection.

TIP

Gain better control when using texture hammers by striking the texture hammer with a deadblow hammer.

 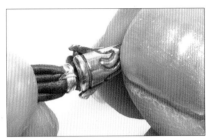 

apply a cord end to multiple lengths

Bind all cord ends with wire. Trim the ends if necessary. Insert the cord ends into the pinch end as far as they will go (you may need to open the pinch end slightly wider than it already is using chainnose pliers). Use chainnose pliers to firmly close the pinch end, making certain to push in the prong sides. (Optional: you can use a small amount of glue inside the pinch end.)

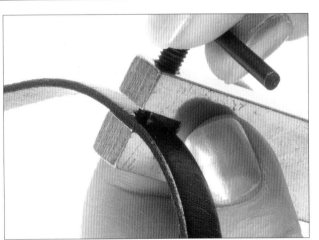 

hole punch tools

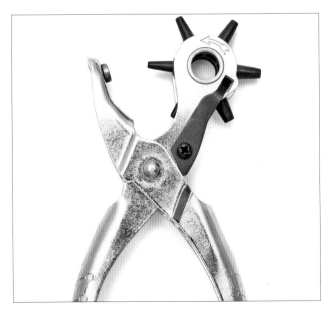

A **two-hole punch** makes holes approximately $\frac{1}{16}$ in. and $\frac{3}{32}$ in. in diameter. A **EuroPower hole punch** will punch holes in seven diameters ($\frac{3}{32}$-, $\frac{1}{8}$-, $\frac{5}{32}$-, $\frac{3}{16}$-, $\frac{7}{32}$-, $\frac{1}{4}$-, and $\frac{9}{32}$-in.). Both of these punches are designed for metal but will also punch leather. A **rotary punch** is specifically designed for punching leather. Its revolving head has punches for six hole diameters: $\frac{5}{64}$-, $\frac{3}{32}$-, $\frac{1}{8}$-, $\frac{9}{64}$-, $\frac{5}{32}$-, and $\frac{3}{16}$-in.

Flat Riveted Button Earrings

This is a fun and simple way to make a pair of stacked, riveted earrings. I love the mix of metals and textures. These are especially fun—they provide nearly instant gratification because they're so quick!

Rivet the daisy spacer to the button (Close-up).

Assemble the earring using two 8mm and one 5mm jump rings and an earring wire.

Make a second earring.

CLOSE-UP ▼

set a two-part rivet
1 Place the bottom of the rivet on the bench block.

2 Place the button and the daisy spacer over the bottom of the rivet.

3 Place the top of the rivet onto the bottom of the rivet and apply a little pressure until it engages. Hold the riveting hammer perpendicular to the piece and hammer the rivet until it is set.

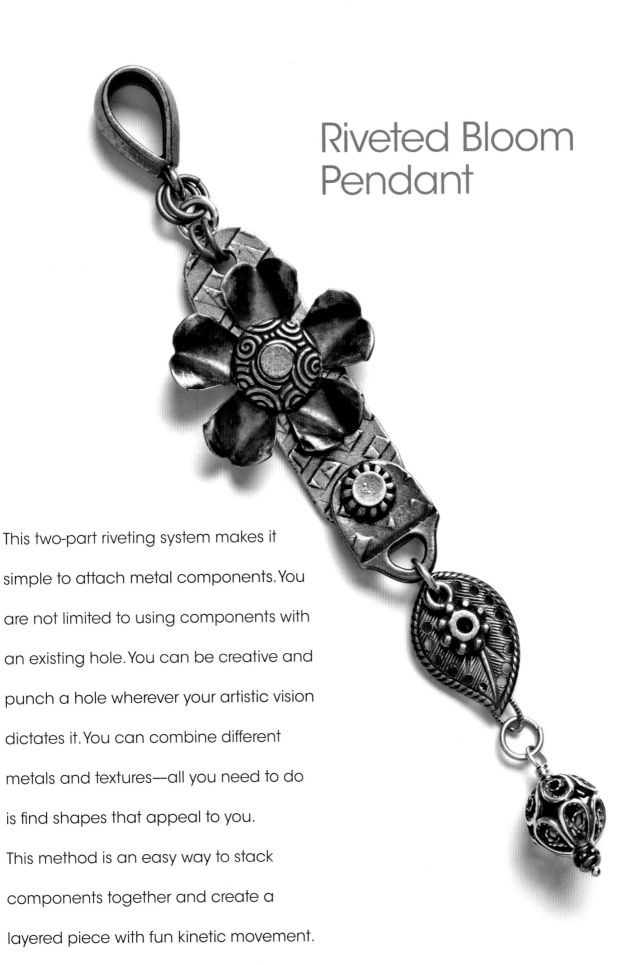

Riveted Bloom Pendant

This two-part riveting system makes it simple to attach metal components. You are not limited to using components with an existing hole. You can be creative and punch a hole wherever your artistic vision dictates it. You can combine different metals and textures—all you need to do is find shapes that appeal to you. This method is an easy way to stack components together and create a layered piece with fun kinetic movement.

STEP BY STEP ▼

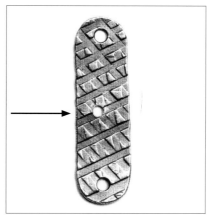
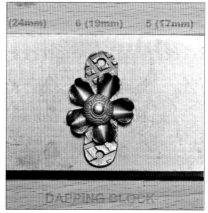

1 Use the large side of a two-hole punch or a EuroPower hole punch to punch a hole in the center of the large link.

2 Line up the bottom of a rivet, the hole you just punched in the large link, the flower component, the beadcap, and the top of the rivet.

3 Put the flat end of a metal punch on top of the rivet. Strike with a deadblow hammer until the rivet holds firmly.

4 Line up the bottom of a rivet, one of the end holes in the large link component, the hole in the strap end, the spacer, and the top of the rivet. Place the assembly on the bench block so the protruding edge of the strap end hangs over the edge, and hammer until the rivet holds (you can stop hammering once the rivet holds, stopping while there is still space between components so that they can move).

5 String a 3mm bead, a round filigree bead, and a metal seed bead on a ball headpin and make a wrapped loop.

6 Assemble the flower link, a leaf link with a charm, and the bead dangle using jump rings and chain (see photo, p. 52).

Crystal Riveted Bracelet

One of the challenges of designing is working out the construction and the structure of a piece. When flat, the crystal element in the center of this design is slightly loose, but once on the wrist, it stretches out and fits the curve of the wrist perfectly. Remember to take into account the movement of the assembly as it is wrapped around the wrist.

STEP BY STEP ▼

1 Connect four 6mm jump rings to the crystal ring.

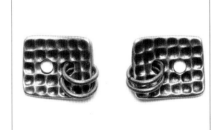

2 Connect two 8mm jump rings through one hole of each button (leaving one hole free).

3 Use single 6mm jump rings to connect all three components.

4 Center the assembly on the flat leather. Use a needle stylus to mark the placement of the open button holes.

5 Use the large end of the two-hole punch to punch one hole.

6 Stack the bottom of the rivet, the leather, the button hole, and the top of the rivet, then carefully hammer until the rivet holds firmly (Tip).

7 Stretch the assembly so that it lines up with the placement of the second hole. Test the fit to be sure the assembly fits the curve of the bracelet when positioned around the wrist. Adjust the placement of the hole, if necessary.

Punch the hole and secure the assembly with a rivet.

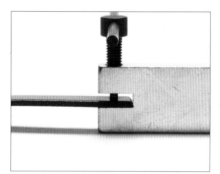

8 Punch a hole at each end of the bracelet approximately 5mm from the end (the black tip of the hole punch is just the right length for this).

9 Align the bottom of the rivet, the strap end, and the top of the rivet so the edge of the strap end meets the end of the leather. Place the strap end on the bench block so that the bottom edge hangs over the side. Hammer until the rivet holds.

Repeat on the other end.

Attach the clasp on one side with a jump ring. Connect three jump rings on the other side, attaching an ornamental spacer to the last.

TIP

To avoid the jump rings when you rivet the assembly to the bracelet, hammer the rivet upside down and suspend the jump rings off the side of the bench block.

Crystal Riveted Necklace

Giving a necklace curve and a drape using riveted flat leather meant that

I had to engineer it creatively. I divided the flat leather into two pieces,

hinging it and giving it a kinetic center cluster. Flexible leather cord creates

a curve at the back of the necklace. All of these elements together create a

piece that drapes well and complements the shape of the neck.

CLOSE-UP ▼

Attach the assembly
Make two components as in
the bracelet (p. 54).

Center a component on one
of the flat leather pieces. Use a
needle stylus to mark the
placement of the open
button holes.

Use the large end of the two-hole
punch to punch a hole. Line up
the bottom of the rivet, the leather,
the button hole, and the top of the
rivet, then carefully hammer until
the rivet holds.

Stretch the assembly so that it lines up with the placement of the second
hole. At this point, you can still adjust the placement of the hole.

When you're satisfied with the placement of the second hole, rivet the
assembly in place.

Use the two-hole punch to punch a hole at each end of the leather
approximately 5mm from the end.

Line up the bottom of the rivet, the strap end, and the top of the rivet, so the
edge of the strap end is lined up with the end of the leather. Place the strap
end on the bench block so that the protruding edge at the bottom hangs
over the edge of the bench block and hammer until the rivet holds firmly.
Secure the other end of the assembly with a rivet.

Make a second assembly with the remaining component.

4 Attach a cord end to each end of the necklace (Basics, p. 32).

5 Use a 6mm jump ring to attach a clasp to one side of the necklace. Use a 6mm jump ring to attach an extender chain to the other side of the necklace. Use an 8mm jump ring to attach a Swarovski drop to the end of the extender chain.

3 Make a lark's head knot (Basics, p. 31) with a double length of leather cord through each strap end.

1 Use a pair of 8mm jump rings to connect one end of each strap assembly (Close-up) to the crystal ring.

2 Use assorted linked jump rings to attach assorted crystal drops to the center crystal ring.

Riveted Button Bracelet

After I made the Flat Riveted Button earrings (p. 51), I wanted to make a bracelet in the same spirit. Because both button holes would have to be used as connector holes, there was no obvious place for a riveted embellishment. Sometimes a challenge like this creates a wonderful solution, which was to punch an additional hole for the rivet.

CLOSE-UP ▼

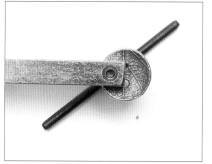

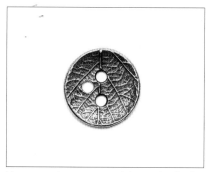

prepare a button for embellishment

Mark the desired location (approximately 3–4mm from the edge and at least 3mm from either hole).

Use the large side of a two-hole punch or a EuroPower hole punch to punch a hole.

Now you have a spot for a riveted embellishment.

TIP

Position the two-hole punch upside down so you can see your mark through the bottom of the punch.

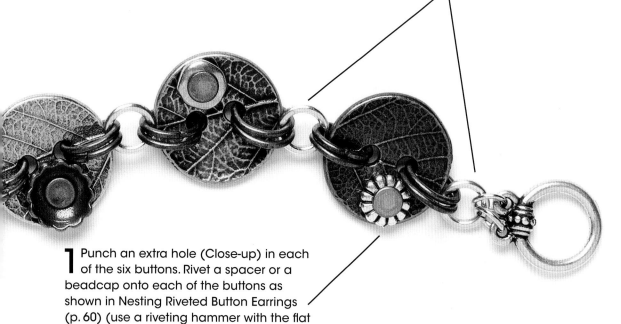

2 Assemble the bracelet using jump rings.

1 Punch an extra hole (Close-up) in each of the six buttons. Rivet a spacer or a beadcap onto each of the buttons as shown in Nesting Riveted Button Earrings (p. 60) (use a riveting hammer with the flat spacers and a dapping punch or dead-blow hammer with beadcaps).

Nesting Riveted Button Earrings

I've always been intrigued with nesting shapes and layering components. Here, the fit and the play of textures of the layered concave components is appealing. This design challenged me to come up with a new way of riveting using a dapping punch to accommodate the curve.

Rivet the beadcap to the button (Close-up).

Connect two 8mm jump rings through the hole in the button. Attach the dangle to an earring wire with a 3mm jump ring. Make a second earring.

CLOSE-UP ▼

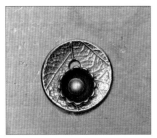 

set a rivet with a dapping punch

Place the bottom of the rivet on the bench block.

Place the button, the beadcap, and the top of the rivet over the bottom of the rivet. Apply a little pressure until the rivet top and bottom engage.

Put the flat end of the metal punch on top of the rivet and strike it with the deadblow hammer.

Place the round end of the metal punch on top of the flattened rivet and strike again with the deadblow hammer.

Flat Riveted Button Earrings
page 51

2 15x13mm metal buttons

2 8mm large-hole daisy spacers

2 two-part rivets

4 8mm jump rings

2 5mm jump rings

Pair of earring wires

Tools & Supplies

Chainnose pliers

Flatnose pliers

Riveting hammer

Bench block

Riveted Bloom Pendant
page 52

40x12mm link

24mm flower component

9mm filigree bead

19mm leaf charm

6mm daisy charm

7mm flat spacer bead

3mm round bead

11º metal seed bead

11mm beadcap

18mm brass bail

Strap end

¾ in. chain

3 5mm jump rings, silvertone

4 6mm jump rings, copper

2 two-part rivets

Ball headpin

Crystal Riveted Bracelet
page 54

14mm Swarovski crystal ring

2 15x13mm metal buttons

8mm large-hole ornamental spacer

4 8mm jump rings, copper

4 6mm jump rings, copper

6 4mm jump rings, silver

2 strap ends

4 two-part rivets

Hook clasp

6–7 in. 10mm-wide flat leather

Tools & Supplies

Chainnose pliers

Flatnose pliers

Needle stylus

Bench block

Riveting hammer

Two-hole punch or EuroPower hole punch

Tools & Supplies

Chainnose and flatnose pliers or 2 pairs of chainnose pliers

Roundnose pliers

Side cutters

Bench block

Deadblow hammer

Metal punch

Riveting hammer

Two-hole punch or EuroPower hole-punch

Crystal Riveted Necklace
page 56

3 14mm Swarovski rings

6 13–32mm Swarovski drops

4 15x13mm metal buttons

35 8mm jump rings

15 6mm jump rings

2 13x4mm pinch ends

4 strap ends

8 two-part rivets

Hook clasp

2-in. chain

8 in. 28-gauge craft wire

2 3-in. pieces of 10mm-wide flat leather

4 10–12-in. pieces of 1mm leather cord

Tools & Supplies

Chainnose pliers

Flatnose pliers

Needle stylus

Bench block

Riveting hammer

Two-hole punch or EuroPower hole punch

Riveted Button Bracelet
page 58

6 17mm round metal buttons

6 large-hole daisy spacers or beadcaps

6 two-part rivets

Two-strand toggle clasp

24 8mm jump rings, copper

7 6mm jump rings, silver

7 4mm jump rings, silver

Tools & Supplies

Chainnose pliers

Flatnose pliers

Riveting hammer

Deadblow hammer

Bench block

Two-hole punch or a EuroPower hole punch

Nesting Riveted Button Earrings
page 60

2 17mm round metal buttons

2 10mm large-hole beadcaps

2 two-part rivets

4 8mm jump rings, copper

2 3mm jump rings, silver

Pair of earring wires

Tools & Supplies

Chainnose pliers

Flatnose pliers

Bench block

Deadblow hammer

Small metal dapping punch

Stamps and Stones Collection

Featuring beach stones and beginning metalworking techniques

BASICS

FINDINGS YOU'LL USE ▼

1 soldered and open jump rings
2 large-hole spacers
3 center-drilled stone beads
4 pin back
5 wire
6 flat braided leather
7 center-drilled glass beads
8 stone pendant
9 silk cord

filing

Use a metal file and file the edge of the cut piece in one direction until the edge is smooth and no longer sharp.

bail-making pliers

Bail-making or looping pliers have round, barrel-shaped jaws in two sizes and are used for making jump rings, consistently shaped earring wires, large curves, and uniform bails from metal sheet or wire.

texturing

A texture hammer has a patterned head and will leave an impression on metal.

Place metal on a bench block and hammer with firm, steady strokes until the desired pattern is transferred to the metal.

Gain control when using texture hammers by striking the texture hammer with a deadblow hammer.

stamping

Create a pattern on metal using a metal stamp: Place the metal on a bench block and strike the stamp with a dead-blow hammer.

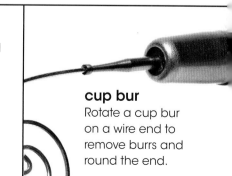

cup bur

Rotate a cup bur on a wire end to remove burrs and round the end.

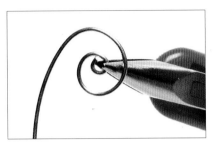

spiral

Use the tip of roundnose pliers to make a loop at the end of a 4-in. piece of wire.

Use the end of chainnose pliers to hold onto the loop while spiraling the wire by hand into an open spiral.

Once you are satisfied with the size of the spiral, use a chasing hammer to hammer the spiral as well as up to an inch of the unspiraled wire. (Do not hammer any part that you intend to bend.)

make a spiral hook clasp

Use the end of roundnose pliers to make a small loop.

Use the end of chainnose pliers to squeeze the loop, leaving only a small opening, then hold onto the loop and begin to spiral the wire tightly.

Once you have reached a loop and a half, switch to flatnose pliers, and continue to spiral the wire until you have two tightly coiled loops.

Make the third/outside loop open.

Use medium bail-making pliers to create a hook in the opposite direction.

Make a tiny loop at the end of the hook and squeeze it closed with chainnose pliers.

Hammer the hook. Pair with a soldered jump ring to make a clasp.

Spiral Beach Stone Earrings

An element as basic as an earring wire can become the focal point of a design. I love the simplicity and sophistication of the large silver spiral with a single stone.

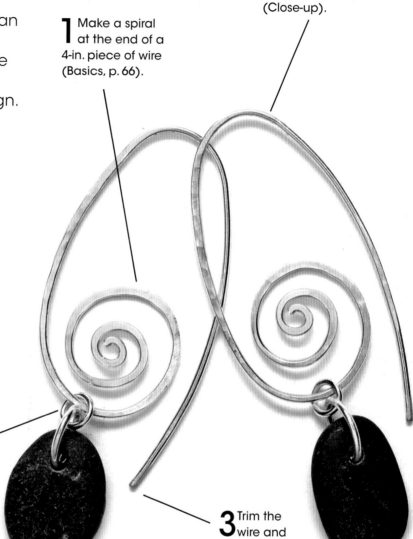

1 Make a spiral at the end of a 4-in. piece of wire (Basics, p. 66).

2 Curve the spiral into an earring wire with bail-making pliers (Close-up).

3 Trim the wire and use a cup bur to finish the wire end (Basics, p. 65).

4 Use jump rings to assemble the earring.

Make a second earring the mirror image of the first.

CLOSE-UP ▼

curve an earring wire with bail-making pliers

Use medium-size bail-making pliers to hold the wire approximately an inch from the spiral and bend the wire downward toward the spiral.

Urban Beach
Stone Pendant

The look of the perfect drilled holes in this beach stone is very modern and it contrasts in such an interesting way against the natural earthy shape of the beach rock. To mirror it in the texturing of the metal in this project, I created the bail to harmonize with the design and also added a handcrafted charm.

STEP BY STEP ▼

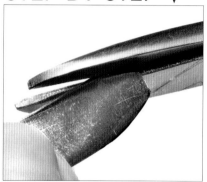

1 Use metal shears to cut a 12x50mm strip of silver sheet. As you cut, round off the corners.

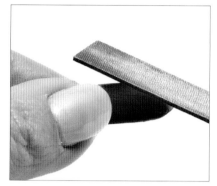

2 Use a metal file (Basics, p. 65) and sandpaper to smooth the edges.

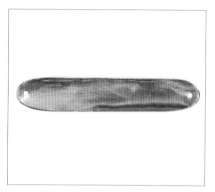

3 Punch a hole approximately 2mm from each end.

4 Use metal punches and texture hammers to texture one side.

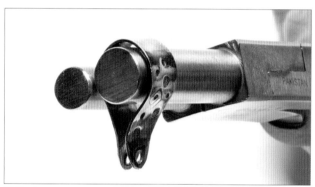

5 To form the bail, slightly bend the ends (approximately 6mm from the end) using flatnose pliers. Then bend the piece using bail-making pliers so that the two holes at the ends line up.

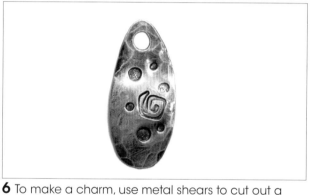

6 To make a charm, use metal shears to cut out a freeform shape approximately 10x20mm and sand the edges. Punch a hole approximately 2mm from one end. Texture as desired. (Optional: Gently dap on a wooden dapping block.)

7 Add patina to both pieces using liver of sulfur.

8 Assemble using a jump ring.

TIP

Wooden dapping blocks are more shallow and have a larger concavity, so they create a more subtle curve.

Pearls & Stones Wrist Wrap

This project combines the matte sheen of riverstones with the rich luster of pearls and the rustic look of braided leather. The handmade clasp suits the handcrafted nature of the piece and completes the design with a perfect finishing touch.

TIP

Measure the cord 1 in. shorter than the wrist size (to allow for the clasp).

Add an extender chain if the wrist size is unknown.

TIP

You can use half-hard wire, you can harden your wire by hammering, or do both to ensure your clasp will endure everyday use.

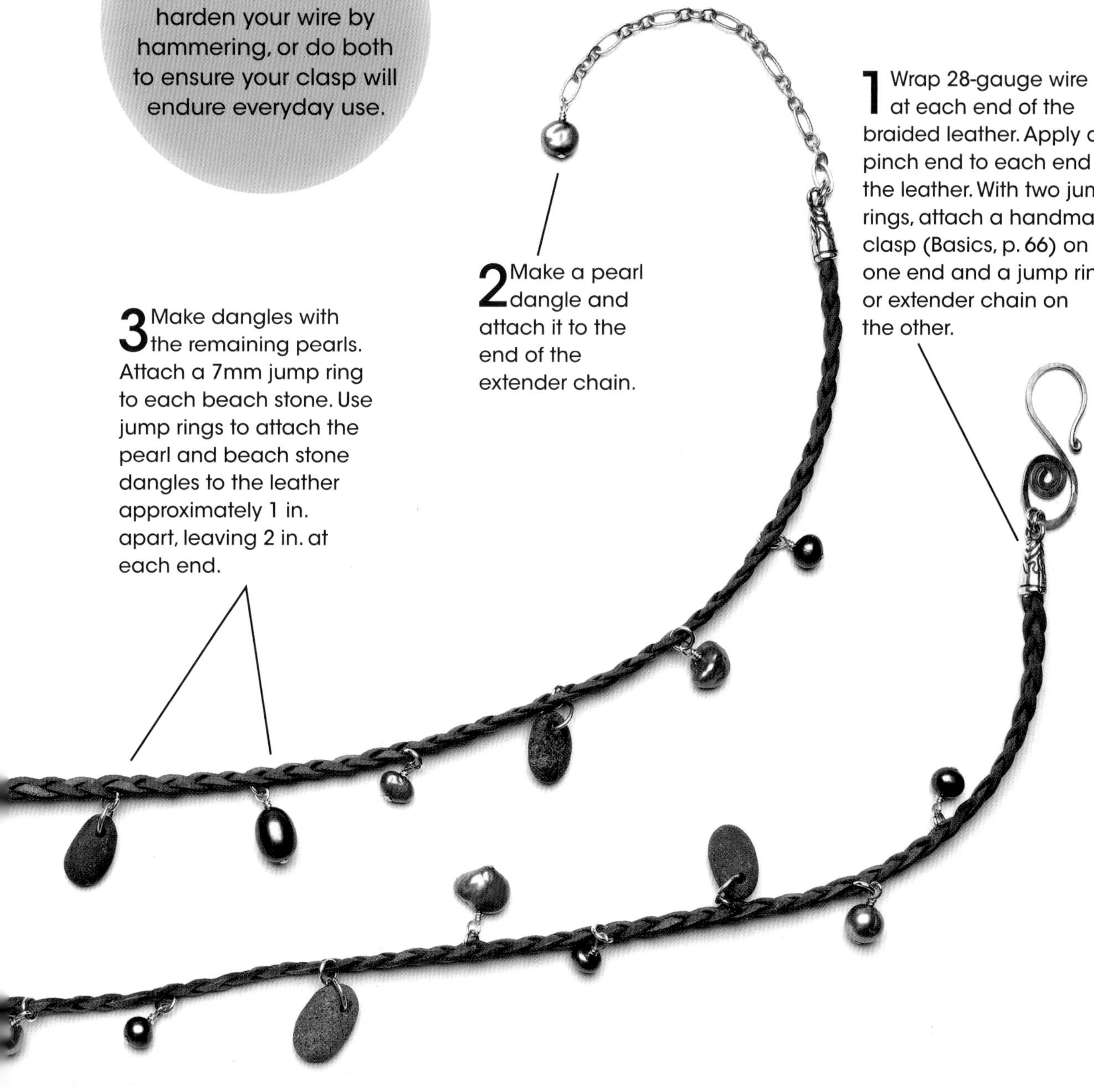

1 Wrap 28-gauge wire at each end of the braided leather. Apply a pinch end to each end of the leather. With two jump rings, attach a handmade clasp (Basics, p. 66) on one end and a jump ring or extender chain on the other.

2 Make a pearl dangle and attach it to the end of the extender chain.

3 Make dangles with the remaining pearls. Attach a 7mm jump ring to each beach stone. Use jump rings to attach the pearl and beach stone dangles to the leather approximately 1 in. apart, leaving 2 in. at each end.

Textured Nesting Pendant

I have always loved picking up stones on the beach. Each stone has its own special color and texture. These pre-drilled stone components are appealing because they are so natural looking. To echo the look, create a custom texture for the metal. Combining round components of varying sizes is a classic design, and stacking textured and untextured elements creates a lovely contrast.

CLOSE-UP ▼

Shaping the pendant
Punch a hole in the center of the silver blank using the larger side of the two-hole punch or a EuroPower hole punch.

Place the silver blank in the largest concavity of the dapping block. Place the largest dapping punch on the silver blank and use the deadblow hammer to strike it. (It's best to lightly strike the blank multiple times, adjusting the punch to round out the shape evenly.) If you're looking for a deeper curve, move the blank to the next concavity and use the corresponding dapping punch. You can continue this process until you're satisfied with the depth of the curve in your piece.

Place the copper gear component on the bench block, position the metal punch, and strike with the deadblow hammer. Use a texturing hammer to add another layer of texture.

Dome the copper gear component in the same way as the silver component.

Add patina to the copper gear component with liver of sulfur.

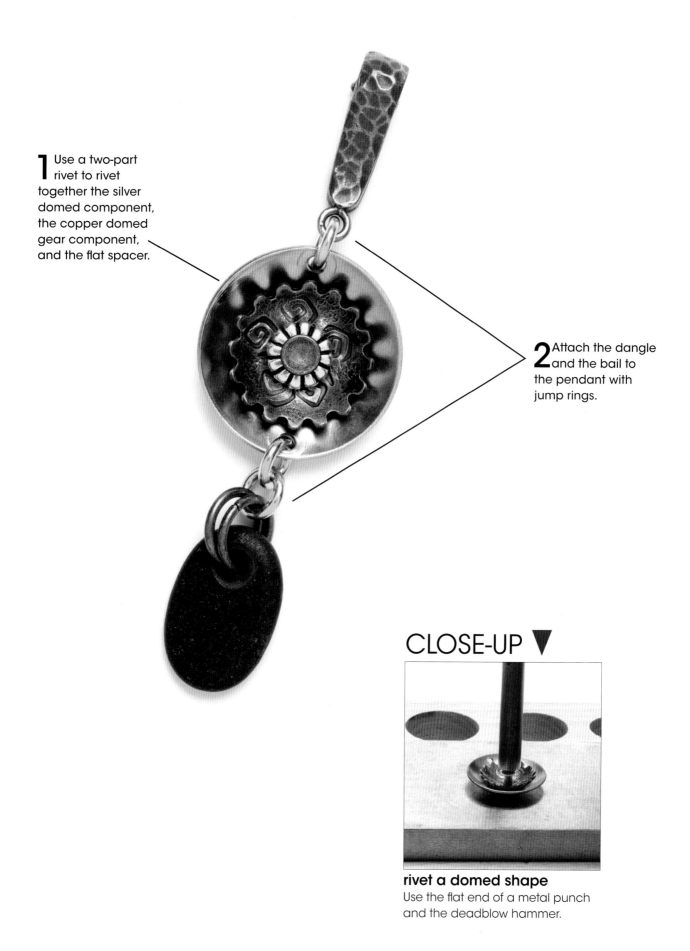

1 Use a two-part rivet to rivet together the silver domed component, the copper domed gear component, and the flat spacer.

2 Attach the dangle and the bail to the pendant with jump rings.

CLOSE-UP ▼

rivet a domed shape
Use the flat end of a metal punch and the deadblow hammer.

Textured Pod Pin

Pods are nature's treasure chests, with mysterious inner realms waiting to be discovered.

I always want to know what's inside them! They are inspiring, and I love creating pieces

that evoke the elegant lines of natural pods.

STEP BY STEP ▼

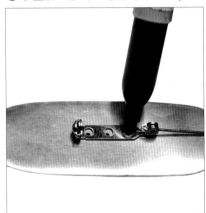

1 Use metal shears to cut a 1x3-in. piece out of copper sheet. Using metal shears again, cut around the corners to round them. Use a metal file to smooth the edges.

Center the pin finding on top of the shape and trace the holes with a permanent marker.

2 Punch holes at the marked spots.

3 Finish the edges by lightly texturing with the chasing hammer.

4 Texture the piece close to the center on one side (this side will be inside the pod) and along the sides on the other side (this side will be the outside of the pod) with texture hammers and a chasing hammer.

5 Begin shaping the piece by rolling the edges upward with bail-making pliers. (Keep the center of the pin flat; be careful not to distort it while shaping.)

TIP

TIP

Hammering and shaping the metal can make it work-hardened. You can anneal (soften) it by heating it with a torch. Use pickle to remove the resulting fire scale.

6 Continue to shape using flat-nose pliers and/or nylon-jaw pliers. If the metal becomes too hard to manipulate, you may need to anneal it (Tip).

7 Add patina with liver of sulfur.

8 Layer a rivet bottom, the pin finding, the shaped metal, a flat spacer, and a rivet top. Use an anvil with the pin straddling the pointed anvil horn and use the flat end of a punch and a deadblow hammer to secure the rivet. Repeat with the remaining holes.

Beach Stones & Glass Necklace

The many colors and moods of the ocean inspired this necklace. I chose traditional colors of beach glass—greens and teals—that echo the color of water. The ribbon complements those colors and also brings its own shades and moods of the sea. The beach stone is mirrored with a beach stone-shaped charm stamped with the name of the necklace for a finishing touch.

1 Leave a 6-in tail, and string 12–15 in. of stones, glass, spacers, and rings on the ribbon, using the stopper technique (Close-up, p. 78) after each set of beads.

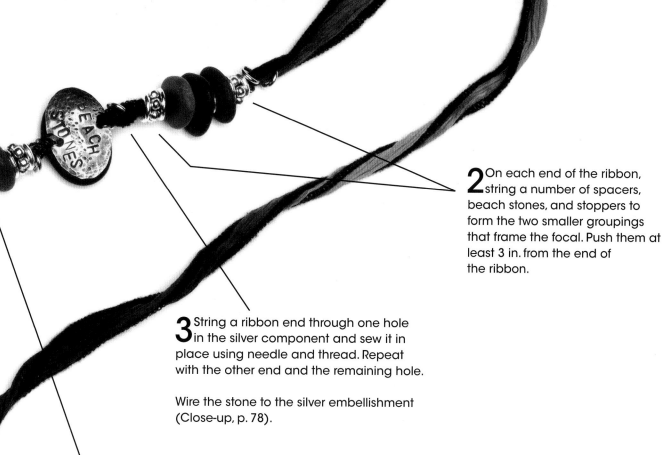

2 On each end of the ribbon, string a number of spacers, beach stones, and stoppers to form the two smaller groupings that frame the focal. Push them at least 3 in. from the end of the ribbon.

3 String a ribbon end through one hole in the silver component and sew it in place using needle and thread. Repeat with the other end and the remaining hole.

Wire the stone to the silver embellishment (Close-up, p. 78).

4 Push the beads in the two smaller groupings toward the silver component and position them so that they cover the sewn ribbon ends. Use jump ring stoppers to hold them in place. Add more jump rings for an aesthetic effect.

CLOSE-UP ▼

the silver stamped embellishment

Use metal shears to cut a shape out of silver sheet that reflects the shape of your focal stone. (Mine is approximately 25x18mm.)

Use a metal file and sandpaper to smooth the edges. Punch holes approximately 2mm from the top and bottom edges.

Use metal alphabet punches to stamp a phrase.

Use a texture hammer and/or a chasing hammer to texture one side of the component. Use a wooden dapping block and a chasing hammer to add a shallow curve to the piece. Shape it so it fits well on top of your focal stone.

Add patina with liver of sulfur.

attach the stone to the embellishment

Cut two pieces of wire and string all four ends through the hole in the stone. String the ends of each wire around the stone and back through each respective loop to form a lark's head knot.

Then use both pairs of ends to connect the stone to the silver component through the holes on each side. Wrap the wire and trim the ends.

CLOSE-UP ▼

stopper technique

Open several jump rings.

Use a needle stylus to pierce a hole through the silk ribbon.

Insert an open jump ring, and close the jump ring. The jump ring will act as a "stopper" and will hold your other components in place.

MATERIALS

Spiral Beach Stone Earrings
page 67

2 10x14mm beach stones
2 7mm jump rings
2 3mm jump rings
20-gauge sterling silver wire cut into **2** 4-in. pieces

Tools & Supplies
Chainnose pliers
Flatnose pliers
Roundnose pliers
Medium bail-making pliers
Side cutters
Chasing hammer
Bench block
Cup bur

Beach Stones & Glass Necklace
page 76

25x20mm center-drilled focal beach stone
10 12–18mm center-drilled beach stones (Jeff Plath)
19 square center-drilled flat matte glass beads (Jeff Plath)
25 10mm large-hole daisy spacers
95–110 assorted jump rings
24-gauge sterling silver wire
Sterling silver sheet metal
Beading thread
Silk ribbon

Tools & Supplies
Flatnose pliers
Chainnose pliers

Side cutters
Metal shears
Bench block
Deadblow hammer
Alphabet stamps
Needle stylus
Wooden dapping block
Needle

Urban Beach Stone Pendant
page 68

44x26mm drilled beach stone (Jeff Plath)
11mm jump ring
Sterling silver sheet metal

Tools & Supplies
Flatnose pliers
Chainnose pliers
Bench block
Punches
Deadblow hammer
Bail-making pliers
Metal shears
Texturing hammer
Sandpaper
Two-hole punch or EuroPower hole punch
Liver of sulfur
Optional: wooden dapping block

Textured Nesting Pendant
page 72

11x17mm drilled flat beach stone
22mm round silver blank
16mm copper gear component

7mm large-hole flat spacer
Copper bail
Two-part rivet
2 8mm jump rings, copper
3 5mm jump rings, silver

Tools & Supplies
Chainnose pliers
Flatnose pliers
Bench block
Deadblow hammer
Dapping block and dapping punches
Texturing hammer
Two-hole punch or EuroPower hole punch
Liver of sulfur

Textured Pod Pin
page 74

3 large-hole 8mm flat spacers
Pin finding
3 two-part rivets
24-gauge copper sheet metal

Tools & Supplies
Flatnose pliers
EuroPower hole punch
Deadblow hammer
Anvil
Metal punches
Texturing hammer
7mm and 9mm bail-making pliers
Metal shears
Metal file
Permanent marker
Chasing hammer
Optional: nylon-jaw pliers
Optional: annealing equipment: torch, pickle, and pickle pot

Pearls & Stones Wrist Wrap
page 70

23 4–6mm pearls
10 drilled beach stones
36 5mm jump rings
10 7mm jump rings
23 headpins
2 pinch ends
3 in. extender chain
6 in. 28-gauge wire
5 in. 18-gauge wire
36 in. flat braided leather

Tools & Supplies
Chainnose pliers
Flatnose pliers
Roundnose pliers
Side cutters
Medium bail-making pliers
Chasing hammer
Bench block
Optional: nylon-jaw pliers
Metal file
Texturing hammer
Chasing hammer
Sandpaper
Two-hole punch or EuroPower hole punch
Liver of sulfur

Tassels and Stacks Collection

BASICS

FINDINGS YOU'LL USE ▼

1   assorted round and bicone crystals
2   wire guard
3   crimp lock
4   chain: cable
5   jump rings
6   chain: long and short
7   chain: rolo
8   flat filigree: round, square, rectangle, flower
9   end cap
10 metal rings

make a tassel
Make a triple loop approximately 3mm in diameter using small bail-making pliers, starting an inch from the end of the wire.

Cut chain as specified in the project directions.

Slide the end link of each chain piece onto the triple loop, distributing the chain equally among the loops.

Use chainnose pliers to bend the long end of the wire so that it's perpendicular to the triple loop.

Use the short wire end to wrap around the base of the longer end (this will make a wrapped triple loop). Trim the short wire.

finish a tassel
Pull the tassel through the endcap. String a crystal onto the wire and make a wrapped loop.

make a stack

Bend the 28-gauge wire in half. String both ends of the wire through adjacent holes of a filigree component. On each end of the wire string a bead, then string each end of the wire, through two corresponding loops of the next filigree component. Continue alternating beads and filigrees until you have strung through the number of beads and filigrees specified in the project directions. String both wire ends through the adjacent holes in the filigree and continue stringing beads and filigrees. Repeat until you have gone around the entire filigree. String each end of the wire through at least one more row of beads.

Trim the ends, leaving an 8–10 mm tail. Bend the tail toward the next bead and use chainnose pliers to bend it again right over the bead hole. Use chainnose pliers to push the end of the wire into the bead.

Note: Material lists will specify the style and quantity of filigree components and the color and quantity of crystals for each project.

attach a wire guard

Wire guards serve two purposes. They provide an attractive finishing for a necklace or bracelet, and they protect the wire from chafing or fraying over time.

String a crimp bead or crimp lock at the end of a beaded strand. String the beading wire through one end of the wire guard.

String it back through the other end of the wire guard, pulling the wire snug against the channel.

String a clasp or loop and then go back through the crimp bead or crimp lock.

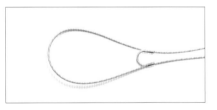

secure a crimp lock

Pull both wire ends snug. Use chainnose pliers to press the tab of the crimp lock toward the bead. Trim the wire tail with wire cutters.

Chain Tassel Earrings

These earrings evoke the wonderful designs of the Roaring Twenties and are reminiscent of flapper dresses and accessories. Asymmetrical splashes of color update the look.

1 Make a tassel (Basics, p. 83) with nine 1¼-in. pieces of chain and a triple loop. Attach crystals to the outside chain pieces of the tassel with wrapped loops. Finish with an endcap and a bicone crystal (Basics, p. 83).

3 Attach two 5mm jump rings to the textured ring. Use a single 3mm jump ring to connect an earring wire to the double jump rings.

2 Use two 5mm jump rings to connect the loop at the top of the tassel to the textured ring.

Stacked Tassel Pendant

The Roaring Twenties inspired this pendant. The iconic tassel, paired with a colorful stacked component, creates a three-dimensional piece with cascading hues. Explore the nuances of color gradation with this beautiful project.

CLOSE-UP ▼

stack

Arrange the crystals into a color gradation from lightest to darkest.

Make a stack (Basics, p. 84), beginning with the lightest crystal color. Continue alternating beads and filigree components according to color gradation until you have strung through eight components and seven pairs of beads.

String both wire ends through the adjacent holes in the filigree components and continue stringing, reversing the order of the crystal colors (so they line up within each row). Finish the stack as described in Basics.

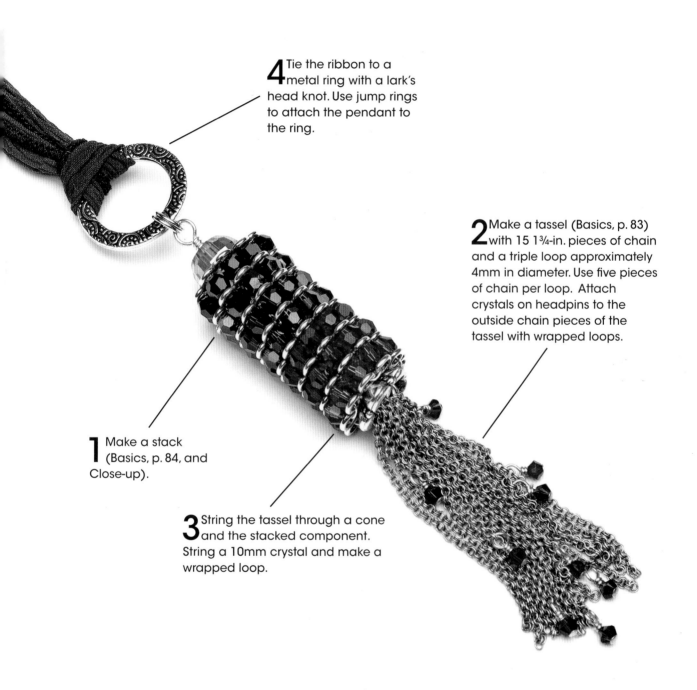

4 Tie the ribbon to a metal ring with a lark's head knot. Use jump rings to attach the pendant to the ring.

2 Make a tassel (Basics, p. 83) with 15 1¾-in. pieces of chain and a triple loop approximately 4mm in diameter. Use five pieces of chain per loop. Attach crystals on headpins to the outside chain pieces of the tassel with wrapped loops.

1 Make a stack (Basics, p. 84, and Close-up).

3 String the tassel through a cone and the stacked component. String a 10mm crystal and make a wrapped loop.

Stacked Spinner Ring

This kinetic ring reminds me of an

ever-changing seascape. Turn the bead

and see the range—from the clear color of

calm water to a very dark and stormy blue.

1 Make a stack (Basics, p. 84, and note). Make a ring base (Close-up).

2 Connect the ring base and the beaded stack with ball headpins (Close-up).

CLOSE-UP ▼

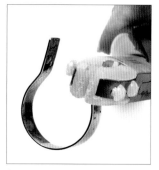

ring base
Wrap a strip of paper around the desired size on the ring mandrel, mark the size, add ½ in., and mark again.

Mark the metal sheet 8mm wide by the length of the marked paper (for example, for size 9: 2¼ in. + ½ in. = 2¾ in.). Cut with metal shears.

File the edges and sand with fine-grit (2000) sandpaper. Texture with a texturing hammer.

Shape over a mandrel.

Use nylon-jaw pliers to slightly bend the sides of the shank until parallel. Mark and punch holes with punch pliers.

CLOSE-UP ▼

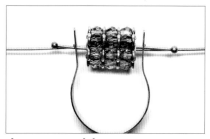

ring assembly
String two ball headpins in opposite directions through the sides of the ring and the beaded stack. Adjust the ball headpins so that there is approximately 3mm between the ball and the ring base on each side.

Bend each headpin end opposite the ball flush against the ring base. Wrap each end around the opposite ball headpin 2–3 times to fill the 3mm gap. Trim and tuck the ends.

NOTE

stack
Make a stack (Basics, p. 84). Alternate filigree components and color A crystals until you have strung three crystals and four filigrees. String one wire end through the adjacent hole on the filigree component, and string color B crystals alternating with filigree. Repeat with color C, D, C, and B crystals. Finish the stack as in Basics.

Stacked Elegance Bracelet

For this bracelet, I've brought together various elements from this collection and recombined them into an eclectic, modern design. It's inspired by vintage style, but it has a modern structure with an asymmetrical layout and a playful re-imagining of a tassel.

4 Finish the end of the flexible beading wire with a wire guard and secure with a crimp lock (Baasics, p. 84). Attach the toggle bar and a decorative ring with two jump rings.

3 String an assortment of crystal beads, spacer beads, and beadcaps.

CLOSE-UP ▼

Stack-tassel segment
String an endcap and a 4mm crystal on one wire end.

Make a wrapped loop.

String an endcap and the stack on the other wire end.

Make a wrapped loop above the stack.

1 Make a stack (Basics, p. 84 and Notes, below). Make a tassel (Basics, p. 85 and Notes). Connect the tassel and the stack (Close-up).

2 Crimp one end of the flexible beading wire to the wrapped loop on the stacked component with a wire guard and a crimp lock (Basics, p. 84).

5 Attach the ring of the clasp to the wrapped loop at the end of the tassel with two jump rings.

NOTES

Tassel

Make a tassel (Basics, p. 83) with 15 2-in. pieces of chain and a 4mm triple loop. Place five pieces of chain per loop. Embellish the chain with 3mm bicone crystal dangles. Make a second triple loop and link the remaining chain ends, placing five pieces of chain per loop. Finish by wrapping the ends as in Basics.

Stack

Arrange the crystals into a color gradation from lightest to darkest. Follow the instructions in Basics (p. 84) to make a stack, beginning with a 4mm round crystal of the lightest color.

Alternate beads and filigree components according to color gradation until you have strung through four components and three pairs of beads. String both wire ends through the adjacent holes in the filigree components and continue stringing crystals and filigrees, reversing the order of the crystal colors (so they line up within each row).

Repeat until you have gone around the entire circle. String each end of the wire through at least one more row of beads. See Basics (p. 84) for finishing instructions.

Reversible Stacked Pendant

In this piece I've built further onto the Stacked Tassel Pendant technique, constructing it with two distinct sides in two different color gradations. This pendant is inspired by Art Nouveau elements in its design, including the way the tassel is suspended and the symmetry of the two hanging crystals. It's also reversible, and the colors in the tassel are complementary to both sides.

CLOSE-UP ▼

NOTE

Tassel

Make a tassel with nine 1½-in. pieces of rolo chain, and a triple loop that is approximately 3mm in diameter. String three pieces of chain per loop.

Finish as in Basics (p. 83), stringing a 3mm spacer bead onto the wire before you pull the tassel through the endcap. (Tip, p. 93)

Reversible stack
Arrange the crystals for one side into a color gradation from lightest to darkest (to avoid confusion, it's easiest to work on one side at a time).

String a piece of 28-gauge wire through the center hole on one side of a filigree component. String a color A crystal and the same hole of another filigree component. Continue to alternate between filigree components and crystals, progressing from lightest to darkest. Use six rows of crystals and seven filigrees. Pull the wire through until it's centered.

String one of the wire ends through the adjacent hole in the filigree component and continue stringing, reversing the order of the crystal colors.

Continue the pattern, using both ends of the wire until you have strung through all five holes on one side.

String each end of the wire through at least one more row of beads. Finish the wire ends (Basics, p. 84).

Repeat for the other side using the second color gradation.

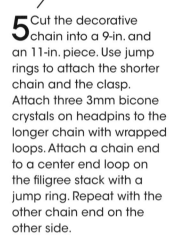

1 Make a reversible stack (Basics, p. 84, and Close-up).

3 Make two wrapped loop 5mm crystal bicone and spacer bead dangles. Use jump rings to connect a 1½-in. piece of rolo chain and the dangles to two of the open loops at the base of the beaded stack.

5 Cut the decorative chain into a 9-in. and an 11-in. piece. Use jump rings to attach the shorter chain and the clasp. Attach three 3mm bicone crystals on headpins to the longer chain with wrapped loops. Attach a chain end to a center end loop on the filigree stack with a jump ring. Repeat with the other chain end on the other side.

4 Attach the tassel to the center link of chain using a single jump ring.

2 Make a tassel (Basics, p. 83 and Note). Embellish the tassel with 10 3mm bicone crystal dangles.

The reverse side shifts from black to pale gray.

MATERIALS

Chain Tassel Earrings
page 85

12–14 3mm bicone crystals

2 16mm textured jump rings

2 endcaps

8 5mm jump rings

2 3mm jump rings

10–12 24-gauge headpins

6-in. 24-gauge wire

2 ft. fine-link chain

Pair of earring wires

Tools & Supplies

2 pairs of chainnose pliers or chainnose and flatnose pliers

Roundnose pliers

Side cutters

Small bail-making pliers

Stacked Tassel Pendant
page 86

10mm round crystal

70 4mm round crystals, 10 each of 7 colors (choose the colors that will gradate from lightest to darkest)

10 3mm bicone crystals

19mm textured ring

8 10-loop circle filigree links

2 5mm jump rings

4 in. 28-gauge craft wire

10 in. 22-gauge craft wire

28 in. fine-link chain

9x11mm cone

10 24-gauge headpins

Silk ribbon

Tools & Supplies

2 pairs of chainnose pliers or chainnose and flatnose pliers

Roundnose pliers

Side cutters

Small bail-making pliers

Stacked Elegance Bracelet
page 90

3 5x8mm rondelle crystal

10x13mm baroque crystal

8mm square crystal

2 8mm bicone crystals

4mm round crystal

30 4mm round crystals, 10 each of three colors (choose the colors that will comprise a color gradation from lightest to darkest)

15 3mm bicone crystals

5 2mm spacer beads

4 10-loop circle filigree links

9mm textured ring

8mm endcap

2 8mm square beadcaps

29x11mm cone

6 5mm jump rings

15 24-gauge headpins

2 wire guards

2 crimplocks

Flexible beading wire

15 in. 28-gauge craft wire

12 in. 22-gauge craft wire

32 in. fine link chain

Toggle clasp

Tools & Supplies

2 pairs of chainnose pliers or chainnose and flatnose pliers

Roundnose pliers

Side cutters

Small bail-making pliers

Stacked Spinner Ring
page 88

3 3mm round crystals, color A

6 3mm round crystals, color B

6 3mm round crystals, color C

3 3mm round crystals, color D

4 round 6-hole filigree components

8x3-in. (approx.) 22-gauge sterling silver sheet

8 in. 28-gauge craft wire

2 2-in. 20-gauge ball headpins

Tools & Supplies

Roundnose pliers

Chainnose pliers

Side cutters

Nylon-jaw pliers

Hole punch pliers

Ring mandrel

Metal shears

Texturing hammer

Bench block

Flat metal file

000 fine-grit sandpaper

Paper

Permanent marker

Ruler

Optional: liver of sulfur

Reversible Stacked Pendant
page 92

5 4mm round crystals in 6 colors (total of 30 crystals), for side 1

5 4mm round crystals in 6 colors (total of 30 crystals), for side 2

4mm round crystal in a neutral color

2 5mm bicone crystals in a neutral color

13 3mm bicone crystals in a neutral color

3mm spacer bead

2 2mm spacer beads

7 12-loop rectangular filigree components

8mm endcap

6 4mm jump rings

15 24-gauge headpins

8 in. 24-gauge craft wire

2 12-in. pieces of 28-gauge craft wire

20 in. decorative chain

16 in. fine rolo chain

Hook clasp

Tools & Supplies

2 pairs of chainnose pliers or chainnose and flatnose pliers

Roundnose pliers

Side cutters

Small bail-making pliers

Acknowledgments

Thank you to my husband, Tony Miech, for his unwavering
support of my work; Lauren Walsh for her writing advice;
and my sons, Zachary and David, for their encouragement
and love.

I thank my editor, Karin Van Voorhees, and the rest of the
Kalmbach staff for their invaluable assistance.

Thanks also to my wonderful store staff members for all
of their enthusiastic help and continual support.

ABOUT THE AUTHOR ▼

Irina Miech is an artist, teacher, and author. She also oversees her two retail
stores, Eclectica and The Bead Studio, in Brookfield, Wisconsin, where she
teaches classes in beading, wirework, and metal clay. Her jewelry designs have
been featured in *Bead&Button*, *Bead Style*, and *Art Jewelry* magazines. This is
her tenth book with Kalmbach Publishing.

Other books by Irina Miech
- *Irina's Metal Clay Collection*
- *Classic Style Fresh Look*
- *Irina's Inspirations for Jewelry*
- *Beautiful Wire Jewelry for Beaders 2*
- *Beautiful Wire Jewelry for Beaders*
- *Metal Clay Rings*
- *Inventive Metal Clay for Beaders*
- *More Metal Clay for Beaders*
- *Metal Clay for Beaders*

Explore wire, beading, and more with Irina

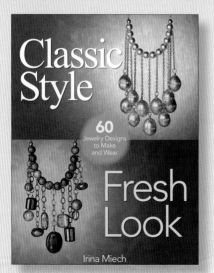